My Life.
My Thoughts.
My World.

Belongs to:

_____

ISBN : 979-8-9861965-1-0

Ladies,

I've been there.

The alarm rings. Time to get up. You wish you could take a walk and enjoy the beautiful morning, but your work schedule is jam - packed.

The hours pass and in each meeting of the day, you've come to believe that you just aren't being heard. Like you're not even there. You wish you had the confidence to speak up more, but instead you keep quiet.

Until today.

This journal provides you with the space to write down your thoughts, motivations, dreams, wishes, desires, pet peeves(wink) and whatever else. Sometimes it takes us getting the thoughts out of our heads and onto the paper for us to see things clearly. This can also be a great intermediary step to having the courage to speak up more.

Even a nominal three minutes a day dedicated to yourself will help you see the beauty that's in YOU, the things in life that you desire to improve and charting a course for what's next.

And always know I'm here rooting for you. If you find on your journey that you could use some guidance contact me for coaching sessions at https://mymentor.life/Katrinahayes or coachingbykatrina@gmail.com

Have a wonderful day and remember to embrace the becoming of you!

XOXO

Katrina

"*Feed your spirit.
Nourish your soul.
Embrace yourself*"

– Unknown

Date: _____

Date: _____

Date:_____

Date: _____

Date:_____

Date: _____

Date: _____

Date: _____

Date:_____

Date:_____

Date: _____

Date: _____

Date: _____

Date: _____

Date:_____

Date:_____

Date: _____

Date:_____

Date: _____

Date: _____

Date:_____

Date:_____

Date: _____

Date:_____

Date: _____

Date: _____

Date: _____

Date: _____

Date:_____

Date: _____

Date:_____

Date:_____

Date:_____

Date: _____

Date:_____

Date:_____

Date: _____

Date:_____

Date:_____

Date: _____

Date:_____

Date:_____

Date:_____

Date: _____

Date:_____

Date:_____

Date: _____

Date:_____

Date:_____

Date:_____

Date: _____

Date:_____

Date:_____

Date:_____

Date:_____

Date: _____

Date:_____

Date: _____

Date:_____

Date:_____

Date: _____

Date: _____

Date:_____

Date:_____

Date: _____

Date: _____

Date:_____

Date:_____

Date: _____

Date: _____

Date: _____

Date:_____

Date: _____

Date: _____

Date:_____

Date:_____

Date: _____

Date:_____

Date: _____

Date: _____

Date: _____

Date: _____

Date:_____

Date: _____